The Job Book.

Ways to: Find a job, interview, get hired, keep a job, get promoted, and be happy.

By Mark Kirby

PO Box 6517

Columbia, SC 29260-6517

All Contents Copyright © 2010

Contents

Finding a job

Finding a job opening is sometimes very difficult but this should not discourage anyone from looking for a job.

The number one and best way for people to find real job openings is through word of mouth.

People who are employed at a company or organization usually know about job openings. An employee may have been promoted, may have moved, or that employee may have found a higher paying job at another company or organization.

The advantage of word of mouth notifications of job openings is that the person being told has the "inside tract" on the job in that the job may not have been sent outside of the company or to some employment agency or web site.

Think about the great advantages of word of mouth job information:

- You immediately know that a job is open and you know what company has the opening.
- You may be one of the first people to find out about the job opening.
- The salary of the job position is usually known.

- You know whom the last person was that held the job and why the job is now open.
- The person telling you about the job opening can also tell you things about the job you need to know before you apply for the job.
- Usually the person telling you about the job will tell you if you would like working for the company.
- You can usually find out if the company will be around in the future or if the company is getting into financial trouble.
- The boss is no secret, the person telling you about the job can also tell you what type of person would be supervising you.
- With a word of mouth job announcement you can feel free to question the person about almost anything that might concern you.
- When you go in for an interview, you are not in the dark about the job or the company that gives you an advantage when you interview.
- The person telling you about the job can be used as a reference and that usually helps you get the job if you are qualified.

There are also some disadvantages to using a word of mouth referral for a job:

- You have to admit to the person or advise them that you are looking for a job.

- If the person that tells you about the job also works for the company, they may expect you to reward them as long as you work there.
- Sometimes word of mouth job information is not accurate and such things as the salary, type of work, reason for the opening, and even if there really is an opening, may not be correct.
- If the person telling you about the job opening does not have the means to inform the individual screening applications about you, your chances may be no better than anyone else and even worse than potential employees referred by a job agency.
- You may be restricted to submitting a resume to "get your foot in the door" for the interview since your interest may be unsolicited.
- Misery loves company, and in rare circumstances the person telling you about the job may be miserable and want company.
- The person referring you may not be a well-liked or a good employee and that can actually hurt your chances for the job.
- Persons applying for a job though channels they did not select may aggravate the Human Resources person.

All things considered, the best way to find a good job is by letting friends and contacts know you are looking.

Most people like to help others find jobs and would not tell someone about a job they would not like themselves.

Tell your friends and other relevant parties that you are looking for a job and to let you know if they hear of any.

A second way to find a job is through classified job listings including job web sites.

Many companies still advertise for jobs in the classified sections of publications although those jobs are usually the lower paying jobs.

In these times, the web has taken the place of printed publications and offers the largest selection of job openings and job offers. The web is also a great way to view classified ads from local or regional newspapers in that most newspapers and publications also offer free access to their classified ads on the web.

By reading the classified ad section of a publication or trade journal including on the web, you can quickly skip over jobs that are not of interest to you for whatever reason.

A major advantage of job web sites and web classified ads is that you can search for jobs in a specific geographic area, a specific type of job, and a specific pay range. By using the web and the job site search function you do not have to waste time on jobs for which you are not qualified or jobs that you do not want.

Web site listings for jobs include such important information as whether or not the job requires travel, whether the travel will be day or overnight, and if the travel will be extensive. Obviously if travel is a problem, you would not consider jobs that require a lot of travel.

The web site listings are full of information and usually allow the job seeker to weed out jobs for which they would not like to apply. Having potential employees not apply for jobs they may not like also helps the job recruiter do a good job and narrows the field for you.

For the best results, you should go to a local job site. Most television stations, newspapers, local publications, and State Agencies have web access to their sites where local businesses and organizations post job openings.

National job web sites sometimes tend to be "generic" in that the job openings may be a way for companies to test the job market or attempt to lure employees to geographic areas that may not be desirable.

Another problem with national job sites is that "junk" jobs can get into the listings and waste people's time and sometimes scam people out of money.

Local job listings tend to be more supervised than national listings.

Advantages of classified job listings (including the web):

- A large selection of job openings.
- The job listing usually has the date the job was listed.
- You can look for a job without anyone knowing.
- Important details about the job are posted so you can decide if it is worth your time to apply.
- Many companies only use classified job ads or web listings to announce external vacancies.
- Once you have produced a resume and application it is very simple to submit it to any potential employer by using the web or email (read below about a disadvantage and warning!) and it does not cost you each time as it would using a postage stamp.
- Employers who are in desperate need of an employee or have a need to fill the job opening immediately will sometimes use the newspaper classified or web ads to get quick responses from local people and hire them.
- You can track jobs to see if they have been open for a long time (why does no one want the job?).
- Many web sites actually retain important data for you such as the jobs you have applied for, when you applied for the job, what you have submitted to the employer, and what actions are being taken by the employer regarding your information (a note such as " under review" or "not qualified" tells you of the status of your job application.)

- Once you have an "account" set up on a human resources or job web site including a resume and application, applying for new positions is as simple as one click on the position ("apply for this job, click here").

Disadvantages of using job classified ads or web sites:

- Classified ad listings are much smaller than they used to be which limits job opportunities for you.
- Sometimes classified ads are used to promote high turnover jobs and recruit unknowing job seekers.
- Due to the cost, classified ads usually offer few details about the job opening and are as short as possible.
- Most companies or organizations do not list their name on classified ads which means you may waste time with jobs you would not consider if you had the facts (as en example an "exciting career" with "unlimited potential" and "prestige" may actually be an ad for a night security guard at a toxic waste dump).
- Many scam artists or even criminals may use classified ads to trick people (an ad for a young woman to be a nanny could actually be an ad to lure young women into a trap).
- Web site ads often share your information (usually they say they will in the fine print) with telemarketing groups, which mean you will receive email spam and unwanted phone calls. Unfortunately the telemarketers will have more

information on you than they could dream of and they may also sell you information to others.

- Scam artists may set up bogus companies on the web job site in order to obtain confidential information on you for identity theft, credit cards, loans, or other criminal acts that can really cause you problems.

- Contrary to popular belief, NOTHING you submit on the web is totally secure and your confidential information that you submitted as an application or resume may be accessed by almost anyone who can steal or hack into the information.

- Many employment agencies disguise their ads to trick you into applying for a job and obtaining the job only to find out later that a large percentage of your pay will be going to the employment agency as a fee.

- A few companies will post a job and list the company as "confidential" - BEWARE!

- When you apply for a job on a job web site you may be competing with people from all over the world

- Sometimes the company using the job web site gets so many applications they simply start ignoring or deleting later applications and only look over the first ones.

- Classified ads including web sites are a great place for people to promote pyramid schemes and "job investment" rip-offs. Beware of so called jobs that advertise huge incomes for doing nothing or that require you invest money for the so-called "job" (also called non-traditional jobs).

VERY IMPORTANT NOTE!

NEVER provide your social security number or birth date to any company or organization that you do not know. If a job web site requires that you submit critical and confidential information to an unknown or little known company do not do it or you will be very sorry. There are many identify theft scammers out there just waiting to get your information and make your life miserable or steal your property electronically. Almost anyone can activate an account on a job site and post fake jobs to steal information. In a test, the author posted a resume on a top national job site and received several scam emails requesting confidential information by way of a complete application (one was from Nigeria) within two days.

A third way to find jobs is through Job Fairs in you city or in nearby regions.

Job fairs are a great way to bring companies and job seekers together in one place.

At the job fair, companies looking for employees will set up a booth or table with a representative where a job seeker can obtain information about jobs, ask questions directly about jobs, and apply on the spot for a job position.

Job fairs are more career oriented in that the employers or organizations are trying to find long time employees that will stay at the company or organization for a long time.

At job fairs the employers are the ones looking for employees and most will actively try and recruit people they are interested in which is far different than jobs found through other sources. Employers will also offer brochures, direct contact business cards, and in many cases incentives for people to come to work for them.

An unusual aspect of job fairs is that the employers are actually competing against each other for qualified applicants so they are less likely to drag their feet on someone they like or would want working for their organization or company.

To find out when a job fair is being held on your area, simply watch your local TV news stations or visit their web site. You can also find out about job fairs through universities, State employment agencies, City government, and advertisements of all types.

A current trend is a virtual job fair. Virtual job fairs allow job seekers to attend a job fair from their computer at home and actually email questions to employers who are waiting to respond to you immediately. Virtual job fairs reduce the time and expenses of attending job fairs but have many of the advantages of the job fair.

Job fairs are a great way for people to find a career path.

Advantages of a Job Fair:

- A lot of employers in one location
- All of the employers are looking for employees or they would not be at the job fair
- You know who you are talking with about potential employment
- Employers have a person available at the booth or table to discuss the company, organization, or issues such as benefits and training.
- You are able to see and talk with an employer and they are able to see and talk with you.
- Fewer employment games are played at Job Fairs in that the participants are trying to recruit good employees.
- If the employer seems interested in you, you have a good chance to get a job with that company or organization.
- Both parties can tell up front if a formal job interview or further contact is worth the time.
- Job Fairs are free and all they cost you is your time.
- Job Fairs are like going shopping for a job in a "job store" and are less stressful than other ways to find jobs in that the atmosphere is friendly and pleasant.

The same tips for interviews in this book apply to people seeking employment at job fairs.

Disadvantages of Job Fairs:

- Job fairs can be very crowded and you may not be able to visit the company or organization you are interested in.
- Sometimes a job fair may not be close to where you live and you may have to spend considerable money on travel to attend.
- Employers who have trouble keeping people and have a high turnover due to the work environment (such as the military, correctional officers, low paying jobs, etc.) or poor corporate attitudes tend to use Job Fairs to lure unsuspecting people to work for them with a "hard sell".
- In tough employment times the huge number of people seen looking for a job and the looks on their faces may discourage you and actually depress you.
- Some companies or organizations use Job Fairs to build a pool of potential employees for future use and may not have current job openings.
- You may be competing against young college graduates and first time job seekers who are willing to take a smaller salary for a job than you can.
- If the person at the booth or table has a quota for new job recruits, they may misrepresent the job in order that they meet their quota.
- If you are not qualified for most or any of the jobs at the Job Fair (and that happens to almost everyone at one time or

another) or if no one seems interested, you may leave the Job Fair thinking you cannot get a job and are "worthless" or the situation is hopeless (NOT TRUE!).

- Job Fairs can be used to glamorize jobs no one really wants or as a public relations platform for a disliked company or organization.
- You may spend an entire day a Job Fair and not accomplish anything.
- Sometimes all the crowds and noise is the least a person wanting a job needs to see and hear.

A fourth way to find a job is through a private or public employment agency.

Employment agencies come in two major types. There are government employment agencies for the unemployed and private employment agencies that make money to help employers fill open positions.

Employment agencies are an important part of our workforce and have been around for a long time.

The main reason employers use employment agencies is to shift the burden of screening and finding potential employees to those who have more resources and time to do so.

While seeking a job through an employment agency sounds simple enough it is not simple and can be very frustrating.

Many employment agencies have quotas for their employees to fill positions. In some cases, quotas can be responsible for agency employees pushing too hard for a potential employee to apply for a job that a particular client of theirs is offering.

An important thing to remember is that the person who is handling your case at either the government or private employment agency may not have your best interests in mind. Think of the employment agency representative as a commissioned sales person who needs to make sales or meet quotas to keep their job and income.

Another possible issue is the person doing the screening at the employment agency.

You really need to stop and ask yourself this question: "If the person screening me is really that good why do they not take one of the good high paying jobs themselves?"

It is not unusual for the person doing the screening to be put off or be jealous of someone's credentials or education if that person is more qualified that the screener. Employment agency employees have been heard to make comments such as "that person thinks they are so smart because they have a degree" or " I am a lot smarter than them and I can't find a good job so why should I try and help them find a job I would want?" It is sad but true in some cases; the person handling your case for the employment agency may not be your friend or may not be trying to help you at all due to personal reasons.

Generally you can tell by the employment agency's representative's attitude if they are on your side or not. If the person is very negative towards you or keeps referring you to jobs well below your qualifications or skills, they are not on your side. If the employment agency representative is not friendly or courteous to you they are probably not on your side either.

The real test of whether an employment agency representative is on your side or not is what happens if you are not interested in the jobs for which they want you to apply. If the representative keeps shoving bad jobs your way and then gets aggravated if you do not want them, you are most likely wasting your time and the time of the representative and should move on.

The final issue about employment agencies is their fee. If the employer pays the fee that is best and shows the agency is legitimate. If the employee is expected to pay a fee (sometimes a lot of money) that would be reason for you to reconsider using the agency or being interested in a particular job. Ask up front!

Most people looking for a job cannot afford to pay a large commission for a job or afford a large deduction from their paycheck until the agency fee is paid in full.

Sadly there have been instances of employment agencies having a scam with employers where the agencies will refer the employee, the employee is hired, the fee is paid, and then the employer terminates the employee. The scam is that the employer gets a "kickback" for offering the job and the same job is open over and over again so the agency and the employer can make money off the scam. This type of activity is rare and illegal, but it can happen.

Sometimes the employment agency may not even be aware of an employment agency scam since it may be made secretly between the employer and a client and may have nothing to do with the policies of the agency. The employer supposedly offering the job may also not be aware in that the fee scam may be made without permission or knowledge on the part of the company. Remember, many corporations are very large and it is difficult to know what all the employees are doing or if they are following company policy.

The point is to be careful and always ask up front if a job has a fee if you are hired, how much the fee will be, how it will be paid, and when it will be paid.

Be careful when signing any contracts with an employment agency and read the contract or agreement carefully. If the employment agency contract requires you to accept a job they (or the employer) offer you or requires a fee or penalty fee even if no hired, you may want to think about not signing such an agreement.

Advantages of using an employment agency:

- High quality jobs and careers with major corporations can be found through reputable employment agencies.
- If you are looking for a temporary or part time position, the employment agency is a great place to look especially if the agency specializes in temporary jobs.
- A skilled employment agency representative will discuss your employment needs and wishes and alert you when a job comes to their attention.
- The pre-screening of job openings by the agency representative can save you a lot of wasted time interviewing for jobs you may not want or with employers that may not want you.
- Even if you have to pay a fee, you could save money in the long run since the agency is doing the work of finding you a job and spending the money to do it.
- A good relationship with an employment agency representative could lead to you obtaining the perfect job and better paying jobs down the road.
- Reputable employment agencies will not accept scam jobs or offer them to people seeking jobs.

- Employment agencies offer large selections of diverse jobs in one place for your review and to help you find the perfect job.
- Discussing a possible job with an employment agency representative is like interviewing for the job without the usual stress of an employer interview.

Disadvantages of employment agencies:

- The fee for finding a job through an employment agency can be very high and could be a financial burden on the person who obtains a job through an agency.
- Some people have a dislike for the idea of having to pay for a job since they are qualified for the job and feel they would be the best person for the job.
- The employment agency representative may not have your best interests in mind or may be more interested in placing a client for commission than finding the right job for you.
- Employers who have a hard time recruiting or retaining employees may use employment agencies to try and keep problem jobs filled.
- Long lines and long waits are not unusual for government employment agencies.
- If you do not take a job your agency representative thinks you should take, the agency may lose interest in you and your quest for a good job.

- In some cases, the employment agency will not tell you the name of the company and only give you an address and date for an appointment. This is done to "trick" clients into going to "junk" jobs.
- Some agencies are not reputable and find ways to scam clients or companies.
- The best jobs often may find their way to friends and family members of the agency representatives (and the representative) instead of clients.
- In dealing with employment agencies you must assume they are in the business to make money first, and finding the prefect job for you may not be their top priority.

A fifth way to find a job is to send resumes to companies or organizations.

You would be surprised at how many job openings there are but companies or organizations do not have the time or resources to put a lot of effort into finding an employee for the opening.

One way to get in front of other people seeking jobs is to compose a good resume and submit the resume to companies or agencies you find interesting as a place of employment.

Generally companies understand that if they receive an unsolicited resume the person seeking employment has selected them as a place the job seeker would like to work.

Unfortunately, most unsolicited resumes end up in the garbage next to the desk of some human resources employee. Many unsolicited resumes may actually be disposed of in the mailroom or by a clerk depending on company policies, which is why no person seeking a job can determine their worth as an employee because they do not get a response from resumes they send out.

Privacy laws protect people to some extent regarding confidential information sent to a company or organization but the job seeker should be aware that once the information is sent out it could end up in anyone's hands so caution is advised as to what information is sent unsolicited and to whom it is sent.

Once a GOOD resume is prepared, a job seeker can select companies and send a resume and cover letter to those companies.

A job interview from an unsolicited resume is not the top source for a job interview but it can lead to a job offer.

Advantages of sending unsolicited resumes and letters:

- Once the resume and letter has been produced it is very simple to send them to all companies of interest to the job seeker.

- Receiving your unsolicited resume may cause an interest in you as a potential employee by the company or organization that received the resume.
- Some companies or organizations do not have the time or money to actively recruit employees or use agencies so those companies or organizations may welcome unsolicited resumes of qualified individuals.
- Postage cost less than gasoline so there are significant cost savings to sending out resumes rather than deliver them in person.
- If the company or organization has a policy to send all resumes received to a person in authority, you may actually have a huge advantage over other persons seeking employment through other sources by sending your resume.
- Check the web site of the company of interest. Most companies have a link to submit unsolicited resumes that will save postage costs and speed up the job-hunting process. Aside from the cost of web access (if you do not use a public library or similar public web access) sending resumes or contacting a company about a job by email is free!
- May human resources professionals remember when they sent out unsolicited resumes to find a job and they may try to help you.

Disadvantages of sending unsolicited resumes and letters:

- The sender has no idea who may actually receive the information or what will be done with the information.
- Many unsolicited resumes or letters are trashed immediately.
- Resumes sent by FAX will definitely anger the company or organization unless they requested the FAX. Unsolicited resumes sent by FAX are considered FAX SPAM.
- Companies and organizations have been known to pass around unsolicited resumes and laugh at the information and make fun of the applicant as a type of "humor".
- At current postage rates, sending out a large number of unsolicited resumes can be very costly and possibly a waste of money.
- Time spent finding contact information for companies or organizations and sending resumes may be better spent utilizing other ways of finding a job.
- Some job seekers may get depressed or feel hopeless if they do not get responses to unsolicited resumes.

A sixth way to find a job is to go out and drop in on companies or organizations. (No-appointment applications and job requests).

This is by far the oldest way for people to find jobs. The job seeker "hits the streets" and drops in on companies or organizations without an appointment.

In general almost all companies or organizations will provide you with job opening information if you ask. Many companies will let you fill out the application while you are there and then submit it to the person that reviews applications for consideration.

There is a lot to be said for dropping in on companies. In some instances the company will actually take you to a human resource official that will talk with you and basically do a short interview. It is more difficult for someone to give you the "brush off" when you are right in front of him or her.

One of the best things about dropping in for job opening information is that the person who screens possible employees can get a look at you, talk with you, and determine if you are the type of person they want working at their company or organization.

Dropping in on companies is also a great way to keep in practice as far as interviewing for jobs and interacting with people in a work environment.

The most important aspect of dropping in for a possible job interview is appearance. If a job seeker does not look their best or is not in the best mood, it could kill the whole reason for dropping in on a company or organization for a job.

While driving around for any reason, if a job seeker sees a company or organization they might wish to work for, they should stop in and ask the person at the front desk for an application.

Advantages of no-appointment visit to employers:

- Gets you in the building and through the door.
- May result in an on the spot job interview
- May make employers think about adding you as an employee or opening a new job position within the company or organization if they like your qualifications.
- Allows you to verify who is getting the information and when.
- Saves you the time of using other job sources.
- Bypasses the usual roadblocks of finding a job.
- Human resource people tend to have more interest in people they have actually met.
- Shows the company or organization you have selected them because you are interested in them.
- Eliminates the usual lines and crowds at other job sources.
- If you are lucky you may have dropped in at just the right time to get a job.
- While unlikely, it is possible the job seeker may be offered a job on the spot instead of having to wait weeks for an answer.
- A good way to connect job seekers with employers.

Disadvantages of no appointment visit to employers:

- Some employers do not welcome people who do not have appointments.
- Job seeker may appear "pushy" or desperate to the employer and not be considered for a job position for those reasons.
- The employer may be turned off by drop in job seekers.
- You have no guarantee the receptionist will forward the information to human resources or give you any information about job openings.
- It can be costly to drive around dropping in on companies.
- Driving to a company and waiting to see or talk to someone may take a lot of time that could be used for better methods.
- Some companies or organizations may simply provide you with an application and tell you to mail it back when completed that defeats the whole purpose of visiting the location in person.
- A great way to discriminate! If for some reason your appearance is not what the company or organization is looking for (age, sex, race, handicap) they can instantly exclude you. It is not quite as easy when the job seeker is using other means to inquire about job openings that can be proved or tracked.

For best results the job seeker should combine all of the methods for finding a job.

No one job-hunting method is best for any particular person or job in most cases.

The job seeker will need to determine which best fits their needs, their personality, and their financial condition.

Job-hunting is like any hunting; you have to have the right tools, a lot of patience, and the will to keep on hunting even if you can't seem to find what you are hunting for.

A good hunter and a good job seeker NEVER gives up.

Using a resume to get a Job Interview.

As anyone who has looked for a job knows, finding a job opening is easy compared to actually getting to interview for the job.

The interview process is critical for the job seeker to obtain a job. It is hard to imagine any job where someone was hired without a face-to-face interview.

As you can imagine, a company or organization will receive many resumes or applications for a particular job opening during normal times however the number of people looking for job greatly increases during tough times.

The number one way to get a job interview is through a resume. Some companies or organizations may want an application first, but all will be glad to get a resume. Your resume is critical to getting a job interview and many organizations require a resume in addition to an application.

The key to getting a job interview is to make sure your resume or application is noticed by the person doing the interviewing or hiring. There are many ways to make your resume or application stand out and give you a better chance at an actual job interview.

Producing a resume that will be noticed.

- Make sure your resume is short and to the point. If your resume has more than one page you will probably hurt your chances at getting an interview because the people reading resumes do not like long resumes. A cover letter can be used but generally should not be used.

- Your resume should be short and to the point but not leave out important attributes you may have. When producing a resume, stick to the important facts such as your education, your job experience, and what makes you a good choice for a particular job. Details such as marital status, children, churches, volunteer work, etc. can be discussed later if needed.

- Produce a resume then tweak it to each job for which you may apply. The general facts of the resume may never change but how your credentials will help each employer will change. As an example, if one of your jobs was similar to the one for which you are applying make that the first job experience information that is listed on your resume. Show the potential employer you have what they are looking for and they need to interview you.

- Use color if possible. With color laser printers being so affordable, it does not make sense not to use color when printing the resumes you will send to employers. Things as as simple as an attractive logo for your name, highlight paragraphs in dark blue, lines separating important information, or telephone numbers in color will make your resume get noticed. Do not use tacky colors, always use professional colors such as gold, maroon, navy blue, or dark green to highlight information or highlight your resume design. Sending poor copies or your resume or black ink only may send you to the bottom of the stack. If you must use an inkjet, use premium inkjet paper and one of the higher resolution settings, however color laser is best. You can also make a color copy of an inkjet printed resume but that limits your ability to customize each resume for a particular job.

- If you do not want to print in color at least use color paper when copying or printing. Color paper such as tan, blue, and gray are good choices for a resume if black ink only is used or you make a lot copies of the resume at a copy service.

- Use high quality paper. Nothing says, "don't really care" as much as a resume on cheap thin paper. Use high quality paper that looks and feels good. Paper such as watermarked (high quality with a barely visible brand name in the middle) is a good choice. Textured papers are also a good choice provided they are not too thick.

- Use good size print. If you try to use a very small size print to put more information on one page you will just irritate the person trying to read your resume. Twelve-point text is best for most purposes. (This book is Twelve-point text)

- Use larger or bold text for critical information such as your name and telephone number. Human resource staff likes to be able to quickly find a resume and phone number to call the person on the resume. Fourteen-point text is good for your name and your telephone number.

- Provide at least two ways the employer can contact you. You should list your primary contact number first and then your secondary number such as a cell phone number. It is a great idea to also provide an email address if you have one but DO NOT provide the email address of an employer, that will make the person reviewing your resume think you use your current employer's resources to do other things than what you are paid to do. There is nothing wrong with providing your employer's phone number if that is the best way to contact you during the day however you should realize it may tip your current employer off that you are looking for a job. When using an employer's phone number always state on the resume it is alright to contact you at that number or when the employer answers the potential employer will hang up thinking they might get you fired or in trouble.

- The design of your resume should be orderly and attractive. The ideal resume is easy to read, attention getting, well laid out, and a resume that quickly shows the potential employer why they should interview you for a job.

- Do not put demands on your resume. Things such as full time, part time, temporary, hours worked, salary, and location can all be discussed during your job interview. The purpose of the resume is to attract the interest of the potential employer and get you through the door. During an interview the potential employer will talk to you about issues that concern you or at the end they may ask "any questions" at which time you can ask your questions.

- When sending the resume, it is best to print the employer's address and your return address on the envelope rather than hand write it. Lasers and inkjets have settings to print envelopes and do a good job.
- Never use goofy text fonts to print a resume. Text fonts such as Times Roman and Arial are the standard fonts that look good and are often used.
- Take the time to fold the resume properly before inserting it in the envelope. Nothing says " I don't care " as much as a poorly folded resume with multiple folds or one that does not fit cleanly into the envelope.

Job Application tips:

- Print information slowly, clearly, and neatly
- Do not overstate your education or qualifications
- Do not lie on an application
- Get to the point, do not get off subject
- Short direct answers work the best
- Provide contact information for references
- Fill out all the blanks that apply to you
- Remember to sign the application

The job interview.

Now that your great resume has done its job and you are called for an interview, there are important things you should and should not do at the interview.

The interview is like a "first date" in that the potential employer and you are getting together to see if both of you like each other. The qualification issue is mostly settled since you provided that information on your resume. The real purpose of the job interview is a face-to-face meeting to see if you will fit into the place you are seeking a job. Many people are hired and considered as finalists by their personality, communication skills, and presentation at the interview.

Tips for a good job interview:

- Make sure you get a good night's sleep before the interview. You do not want to go for the interview looking tired or worn out. Never go on a job interview after partying all night or when sick.
- Dress appropriately for the interview. Your clothes should be pressed and sharp, not wrinkled and floppy. A sport coat, dressy trousers, a solid color shirt, and a subdued tie are the most common clothes for a man's job interview. For a woman, a dignified skirt (not too short), a modest blouse, a

sport jacket or coat of some type, and nice shoes are most common. Women may wear pants provided they are dressy and not too tight. Dark colors such as navy blue work well with women and men for job interviews.

- Men should make sure their hair is neat and combed and women should also make sure their hair is neat.
- Men and women should brush their teeth and floss before an interview. Many jobs have been lost due to food in the teeth and garlic breath (really!). Breath spray is all right, but sometimes the interviewer may think the person is trying to hide something such as alcohol consumption. A good choice to freshen the breath is to use a mint mouthwash not too long before the interview. Use of a mouthwash that smells like medicine is not a good idea.
- If you are a smoker, do not smoke right before the interview and do not wear clothes that smell like smoke. These days employers are tending not to hire smokers if they know the person is a smoker and non-smokers can smell if a person is a smoker.
- Make sure your hands are clean and your fingernails trimmed and clean.
- While it may sound funny, check your nose for things that might offend the person conducting the interview.
- Polish your shoes, most interviewers look at a person's shoes to see if that person cares about their appearance.
- Stand tall and walk with dignity.

- Never go into interview acting depressed or desperate. If you are depressed or desperate (or both) you must act like you are not.
- Smile
- Use a firm handshake but not too firm when meeting the job interviewer. If the person conducting the interview is a woman, it is proper to shake hands with her so feel free to extend your hand while you greet the person prior to the interview.
- Be friendly but not too friendly.
- Stay away from personal views or comments unless the person conducting the job interview brings it up. Think first!
- Do not get involved with politics, sports, or religion. If the interviewer brings it up try to politely change the subject or just listen to what they have to say without comment.
- Never argue with the person conducting the interview or preach to them.
- Try not to be nervous. There is no reason for you to be nervous if you believe the company or organization really needs you as much as you need them. Always remember you are equal to everyone and no person is better than you.
- Stick to the interview. Nothing bores a job interviewer more than someone pushing his or her personal problems on the interviewer. Sympathy rarely gets anyone a job.
- Stay still in your seat during the interview. Do not jump around, tap your feet, move your legs constantly play with a

pen or paper, clear your throat constantly, move your hands over your face, or other similar distractions.

- Be prepared for the interview. Know your facts and make sure they are the same as your resume facts.

- It is not a bad idea to practice the interview with someone or do a mock interview while looking at yourself in a mirror. If you have a video camera is it a great idea to make a video of yourself in a mock interview so you can see how the other person sees you.

- Do not eat candy, chew gum, or try to smoke during an interview.

- Women should not wear heavy makeup like they are going out at night. Women should not go into an interview without wearing any makeup.

- Wearing short skirts, tight pants, low cut blouses, or tight blouses is not usually a good idea for a woman who is interviewing for a job. Of course there may be some jobs where dressing to attract men is appropriate, but the person seeking the job will have to be the judge. If the person doing the job interview is a woman and the woman interviewing for the job is "dressed to kill", the interview is over before it begins.

- Men slicking back their hair with hair slick is not a good idea.

- Too much jewelry is not a good idea.

- Answer interview questions with specific answers and with confidence. Do not ramble on when answering a question in that the interviewer's time is valuable to them.

- Don't act silly of goofy. When someone interviews for a job and they act too silly or giggle, the interviewer may suspect that person is on drugs.
- Never tell the interviewer you are "nervous" since they already assume that.
- Look at the interviewer, do not let your eyes wander around the room while they are talking or it will make you look like you are not really interested in the job. When appropriate, look the interviewer in the eyes but don't overdo it.
- There is nothing wrong with saying you like the company, the building, the location, or what the company does but do not go overboard with compliments.
- Answer all interview questions truthfully. If you hide critical information and you are caught later, you may be fired.
- When the interview is concluded do not forget to thank the person for the interview and offer to shake their hand. It is a good idea to tell the interviewer you enjoyed meeting them and hope to hear from them about the job. The end of the interview is a good time to ask when the job will be filled so you will know when to forget about that job (sometimes the first choice does not take the job or does not work out so you may still get the job after the job closes but that is not usually the case).
- Even if you do not get the job, each interview is great practice for the next job interview so your time is not wasted. Always think back on the interview and be honest with yourself. Remember the things you did in the job interviews

that were not good and try not to repeat them in the next interview.

- Remember you are important, and the person doing the job interview is no better than you are even though some act that way. When called in for an interview there is no reason to be nervous or scared.

- It's just a job interview, not the end of the world. If the job interview does not go well it is probably for the best.

Starting a new job.

Congratulations. You have made it through the job seeking and job interview process and have been hired.

The first day and month on a job are the toughest for everyone.

We all like to think we are ready to do a great job when hired and probably will, but there are ways to make sure the new job goes smoothly.

Remember, the first six months of the job are critical in that the employer uses those months to evaluate your performance and decide if you are the right fit for the company or organization. Most employers call the first six months a probation period in that you are being watched and graded on how well you do your job. The good news is that after the probation period you do not have someone watching every move you make and while your job is not secure it is more secure than during the probation period.

One of the biggest reasons for employees not working out in a new job is trying too hard. When people try too hard to please the employer they usually get into some type of trouble.

While these tips may not include all the reasons for new employees (or current employees) getting into trouble, they are things no employee should do.

Things NOT to do in a new job (or current job) include:

- Doing things you are not qualified to do to impress the boss.
- Trying to be too friendly and spending too much time talking with fellow employees.
- Slacking off since you got the job.
- Thinking you know more than someone else who has been at the location for a long time because you are more educated or experienced than they are.
- Acting like you are better than everyone else.
- Flirting with men or women on the job.
- Coming in late.
- Asking for time off in the first six months unless it is absolutely critical.
- Calling in sick, especially on Mondays.
- Roaming the halls or not being at your designated location during work hours.
- Taking extended lunches.
- Listening to gossip.
- Hanging around negative people and people who cause trouble.
- Being loud or laughing a lot like you are at a party.

- Trying to do work too fast instead of doing quality work. Try to find the middle road of fast and quality work.

- Excessive sucking up to the boss. Other employees and some bosses do not like suck ups and doing this will cause you trouble.

- Not dressing properly. Stick to the dress code and make sure you are always presentable.

- Using employer resources for personal use. One of the biggest offenders is using the computer at work to access the web for personal use. Most organizations track usage of the web and read emails.

- Spending too much time on the phone conducting personal business or talking to friends and family.

- Eating at your desk or job location excessively. Break rooms are for eating. Your job location or station is not your lunch or break area unless you are told you cannot leave.

- Taking breaks that exceed the time allowed.

- Taking too many or too long "smoke breaks".

- Not showing up for meetings or training.

- Not volunteering when you are expected to volunteer for certain events.

- Arguing with fellow employees.

- Using an abusive tone or language with your supervisor.

- Making a lot of excuses when you do something wrong (admit you made a mistake, ask what you did wrong and how you can prevent if from happening again, and move on).

- Horseplay. Work is work and play is play. Horseplay at work causes job injuries or damage to the workplace and will usually result in your termination if caught.
- Making racial, sexist, hate, or other politically incorrect comments. Keep your personal views to yourself while at work.
- Associating with co-workers after work during the probation period. If you have a falling out or fight after work with a co-worker it will follow you to work and cause problems and cost you your job.
- Dating co-workers. If you will die without dating a co-worker, find another job then date them. Most inter-office dating ends up with one or both parties losing their job.
- Dragging your sick child to work is never a good idea unless you have permission and it is absolutely the only way to handle the situation. If you bring your child to work too many times you will probably end up losing your job.
- Stealing. Don't steal from the person who provides you a paycheck. Only a total jerk would steal from their employer. Stealing will not only result in instant termination, you could be arrested.
- Drinking, doing drugs, or showing up for work in such a condition will result in immediate termination. Do not even have one beer at lunch unless your boss is with you and suggests it. It is best to decline drinking alcohol at any time during work hours. Remember your boss usually has a boss.

- Women wearing clothes that are too revealing. Most women who do not dress appropriately are sent home to change but if they do it again they may be terminated. Men can also get into trouble for dressing inappropriately.
- Not holding your temper. Lose your temper and throw a tantrum a few times and you may lose your job. Take a moment to relax and get over whatever is making you angry.
- Taking time off. One of the biggest mistakes a new employee makes is asking for excessive time off before they have even earned any vacation time.
- Not listening.
- Thinking you always know the best way to do something.
- Trying too hard and making mistakes because of it.
- Sleeping on the job. Being caught asleep on the job is a great way to lose a job.
- Fighting with your spouse or boy/girl friend at work. If your significant other comes to your place of employment and causes a disturbance you may lose your job.
- Borrowing money from co-workers. If you borrow money from co-workers and cannot pay them back and they tell the supervisor, you may be fired.
- Harassing other employees. Due to liability reasons employers do not tolerate sexual harassment or other types of harassment, and they will fire you for doing those things.
- Hate speech. Trashing any group of people is not part of the work environment and in most cases will cause you to lose your job.

- Listening to hate or political radio shows. Leave the hate at home. If the radio talk show offends other employees you will have problems. Remember the person on the radio is not controlled by you and they could say anything at any time and draw attention to the listener (you!).
- Turning up your radio too loud. Don't disturb others with you radio, it causes problems.
- Being discourteous to clients or customers. If you treat a customer or client poorly they will likely complain to the top person and you will be reprimanded for it. If you have a habit of losing customers or clients you will lose your job.
- Walking around with a portable device and earplugs in your ear looks bad and could be a safety hazard.
- Not reading the employee manual. How can you know what to do and what not to do if you don't take the time to read the employee manual?
- Not reading the procedure manual. The best way to violate company procedures is to not read the procedure manual.
- Arguing with the boss. Unless the boss tells you to do something totally unsafe or illegal, just do it.
- Not wearing safety equipment or disabling safety devices.

There are many positive things a new employee can do when starting a job:

- Show up a little early every day. Showing up early shows you want to be there. Don't show up too early.

- Ask questions if you are not sure about a procedure or task.
- Dress well and always have a good appearance.
- Be courteous to other employees.
- Try to remember the names of your co-workers. People appreciate your knowing their name.
- Keep a positive attitude at work no matter what.
- If possible double check your work so you do not make too many of the usual mistakes a new employee makes.
- Keep your desk or work area clean and not messy or disorganized.
- Say hello to persons you pass in the hall or work area and greet them with a smile.
- If someone asks for your help and you are not exceeding your job duties, you should help them.
- Try not to rush out the door at quitting time. Organize your desk and work area so it will be clean after you leave and when you return the next workday.
- Take breaks in the break room so you can get to know other employees and they can get to know you.
- If the boss asks for volunteers you should volunteer if possible and appropriate.
- Keep copies of inter-office memos so you can refer to them later if needed.
- Read carefully all manuals that are given to you.
- Be polite to everyone. Treat others as you would like to be treated.

- Take interest in company events and attend if you can do so.

- Be confident around your boss and try not to be nervous. Supervisors like employees who do not act nervous or insecure.

- Offer suggestions to reduce costs or improve profits but be careful not to go overboard.

- Follow all safety rules and procedures and use safety equipment.

- Get familiar with the entire company and department locations so you will know where to go if your boss asks you to visit another department. Do not be afraid to ask if you do not know where a department is located.

- When driving a company vehicle, make sure you are courteous to other drivers including those who are not courteous to you.

- Avoid job accidents. Be careful and obey the rules.

- Rather than ask several times, make sure you fully understand instructions the first time.

- Don't bring your personal problems to work.

- Do not be afraid to ask for help if you need help doing your job and always thank the person for helping you.

- Get plenty of sleep during a workweek so you will show up to work rested and looking good.

- Try not to consume alcoholic beverages during the workweek if possible.

- Try to keep minor health issues to yourself such as headaches etc. unless you think it is a medical emergency or it may cause a work accident.
- Be happy at work and let it show that you like your job.
- If the job troublemaker tries to put negative thoughts about the company in your head, simply tell them with a smile you have to get back to work and leave.
- If you see litter or junk that should be disposed of, pick it up and dispose of it even if you did not cause it.
- Let those in charge know you like your job and the company but don't overdo it.
- Make sure you park you car in the proper place and not someone's designated parking space.
- Say positive things about your company and job even when talking to people after work hours. Good things you say may get back to the company or organization.

Ways to be a great employee.

Now you have been hired for a job. The next question is how can you do well at your job so you can keep the job and please your employer.

Everyone wants to do well on the job.

The benefits of doing a good job are obvious and include pay increases and promotions.

What may not be so obvious is how to do a good job and what things you need to be aware of to do well at your job.

People who do not like where they work or do not like the job they are doing rarely do well because they usually don't care. Very few jobs are the greatest job a person has ever hoped for, but most jobs are not the worst either.

The most important aspect of doing well at your job is your attitude.

It is often difficult to keep a positive attitude about a job, but a person's attitude is theirs and theirs alone. No one can force an attitude on a person. As the saying goes "it is all in your mind" and that saying is true. Your job may be dirty, hard, low paying, have long hours, bad bosses, poor working conditions, or other undesirable traits but it still puts food on the table.

There was a person at one work location that never seemed to get upset and never complained about the job no matter how bad things got. This person was always cheerful and never said bad things about the company. The employee was rarely out sick and never late for work. The person was a model employee. When the other workers would ask their fellow employee why he never got angry or disliked his job he would answer in one of several ways. His usual answer would be "hey, it's only a job", "don't let it get you down" and the other answer would be "they can kill you but they can't eat you". The latter would always get a laugh.

The point is that your job is what you make of it. The job is the job and cannot be changed. What can be changed is your mental attitude towards the job. If you go into work thinking the job stinks, the job will stink. If you go into work thinking the job will be fine it will be fine. If you go to work each day and think the job will be great it will be great.

Employees who have a good attitude about their job or life in general always do well, and in most cases do better than other employees who do not have a good attitude.

Ways to be a great employee:

- Listen. Always pay attention to your supervisors and listen to what they tell you.
- Pay attention. Pay attention to what you are doing, do not let your mind wander on different subjects.
- Care. Care about your job and the things you do at your job.
- Look. Look for ways to do your job better and ways to help the company or organization.
- Attitude. Keep a positive attitude at all costs. Negative attitudes do nothing but hurt you and your health.
- Be loyal. Your employer pays you to do a job and they have the right to expect you to be loyal to them and care about them and their success.
- Be friendly. Everyone likes friendly people. Friendly people interact better with their fellow employees and usually do better at their jobs.
- Keep your eyes open. If you see unsafe conditions that may hurt you or your fellow workers, report them to the proper people. If you notice things that might hurt your employer you should also report them using proper channels.
- Do your job. You get paid to do a job. Your employer has every right to expect you to work for your pay and to do your job well.
- Avoid conflict. If there is any way to avoid conflict in the workplace you should do so.
- Don't gossip. Employers do not like people who gossip.

- Stay away from troublemakers. Employers tend to group people together based on whom they associate with. If you hang around negative people or troublemakers employers will label you as a trouble employee.

- Don't be mean spirited. Mean people rarely advance or do well in life.

- Be respectful. Always respect your fellow employees and treat them as you wish to be treated.

- Do not make fun of employees. Never make fun of other employees or their mistakes, it will tend to come back and bite you!

- Help make the workplace pleasant. Helping clean the break room, decorating your space, or making coffee for the group usually gets noticed by management

- Accept your salary and be thankful for the job. You knew the salary when you took the job so it does nothing to complain about your pay. You have a much better chance at a raise if you do not complain about your salary.

- If your company has picnics or company sponsored gatherings you should attend and enjoy them. Management is always at company events and takes notice of who attends.

- Attend training sessions. Even if you are not required to attend, training sessions help make you a better employee and help expand your job knowledge.

- Keep notes of important procedures. People sometimes forget a procedure if they do not do it on a regular basis. As you learn a new procedure take the time to write the procedure in a notebook. A notebook with important procedures is a great way to refresh your memory to keep you productive and informed. Update your procedure notes as needed.

- Be nice to the boss. The boss is human too and likes to know he or she is appreciated. Always try to smile when you greet the boss or a top official.

- Wear company apparel. If your company provides you with free logo shirts, caps, or jackets and you are not required to wear them, you should wear them anyway. Show you are proud to work for the company or organization.

- Take the time to tell your boss or others that you enjoy you job.

- Before you start work each morning (or shift) think about ways you can do the job better.

- As you leave work take time to think about things you could have done better and try to do better the next day.

- Accept criticism with dignity. Some bosses don't know how to point out problems or mistakes so don't take it personally. When the mistake or problem is brought to your attention take it as a suggestion on how to do your job well and not an attack on you. After all, if the boss did not care about you as an employee they would not point out your mistakes they would simply fire you.

- Remember you are no better than anyone else. Never look down on other employees because of what they look like, their salary, or the job they do. The housekeeping crew is critical to the workplace and they should be treated with the respect as the President of the organization.

- Contribute to donations such as charities, employees needing financial assistance, or gifts for the bosses. The little bit of money saved by not giving will make you eventually feel bad. If you give, you will feel good and it will show.

- Do everything within reason to make the workplace a good place for everyone including you.

- Take care of your employer's property. If your employer thinks enough of you to provide you with equipment or furniture you should care enough to not damage or abuse it. If your company provides you with a vehicle make sure it is always clean and serviced just as you would want your car to be.

- Stay organized. If everything is organized well and easy for you to find when you need it you will do your job better.

- Stay focused on your job. Try not to let your mind think about things other than the job when you are at work. You will have plenty of time to needlessly worry about things after work.

- Don't take the job too seriously. A job is just a job. Do the best you can and constantly try to improve. Life is life and a job is just a job. You can get another job but you can't get another life. If you put things into their proper perspective you will be a better employee.

- Always remember no one is better than you so there is no need for you to get upset or angry if someone tries to pretend they are better than you. If a boss or co-worker gives you a hard time it is their problem not yours.
- Be thankful you have a job; many people do not have a job.

Common grounds for termination.

Now that you have a job your goal is to keep it.

There are many ways to lose a job but if employees follow a few simple suggestions they have a much better chance of keeping their jobs. Ways to keep a job are basically the same as ways to be great employee but there are some additional rules apply to keeping a job.

While the list of some common grounds for job termination may seem long, it should be known by all employees and is easy to remember. The order of the list has no significance in that any one or the listed events could result in job termination.

Doing the following things may get you reprimanded and be placed in your personnel file, hurt your chances for promotions, or even get your terminated from your job. If you want a better chance at not being terminated learn the list and be careful.

- Never threaten your boss
- Do not lie to your boss.
- Do not threaten to quit unless you actually plan to quit.
- Do not go around the company making derogatory comments about your supervisor or the company.
- Do not do anything illegal on the job.

- Do not get arrested for any reason on or off the job.
- Do not let bill collectors call you at work or contact your supervisor.
- Do not argue with family members (including your children) on the phone while at work.
- Do not have romantic affairs with co-workers especially supervisors.
- Do not try to increase amounts claimed on expense accounts to get extra income.
- Pay all of your taxes, do not try and cheat the IRS or your employer may become involved.
- Never use your job for a corporate or business discount on personal items unless you have been authorized to do so.
- You should not find a place to hide to avoid work assignments.
- Practical jokes do not belong in the workplace and can cause injuries.
- Inappropriate touching of fellow employees is usually grounds for immediate termination.
- If you lied on your application about education or job credentials you will most likely be terminated if caught so be truthful.
- Striking a fellow employee will result in termination unless you can prove you did not start the incident and had no choice. Generally there is no excuse for striking your boss.
- Never consume alcohol or take illegal drugs on the job.

- Do not use the Internet for personal use especially visiting pornographic web sites.
- Do not use company equipment of any type for personal use, especially vehicles.
- Do not "borrow" company property without permission first.
- Do not speed in company vehicles or drive recklessly.
- While driving or riding in a company vehicle never make rude or obscene gestures to other motorists.
- While customers may sometimes be hard to deal with, you do not have the option to be the same way with them. As few as one customer complaint to the right person may get you terminated depending on the circumstances.
- If things do not go your way do not throw tantrums on a regular basis. Employers do not want to keep unstable employees.
- Never bring a weapon of any kind to the workplace.
- Do not tell others about employee information that is confidential either inside or outside of your work place. There are laws protecting an individual's rights to confidentiality.
- If you are told confidential company or organization information do not repeat it outside of those in the company who are authorized to know.
- Pay child support if you are ordered to do so by a court.
- If you are overpaid bring it to the attention of the accounting department immediately.

- In most work places using curse words on the job on a regular basis may get you terminated. Using certain slang or curse words WILL get you terminated.
- Never make fun of other employees especially those that are handicapped, foreign, or different than other employees.
- It is best not to tell offensive, dirty, religious, or political jokes at the work place.
- Do not blame someone else for something you did, it will catch up with you and make matters worse.

Use your common sense when it comes to what you can or cannot do at the work place. Most companies or organizations have employee manuals but they may not address all issues. A good rule of thumb is if you would not do something in church or you think it might be wrong, do not do it at work. You are not a child, you know right from wrong.

Ways to advance at your work place.

Everyone wants to advance at work and get promoted.

There are certain traits shared by employees who earn promotions and those traits are shared in this chapter. You can also use your imagination to find additional ways to earn a promotion but be careful not to go too far. Trying too hard to earn a promotion can hurt you worse than simply doing your job to the best of your ability.

The following are some traits employers look for in promoting employees:

- Be dependable. Be an employee your employer can count on. Dependable employees always get noticed and have a good reputation within the company or organization. Dependable employees are willing to do their job as required and show up for work without any supervision if needed. Dependable employees are where they are supposed to be and when they are supposed to be there at all times.
- Be trustworthy. Employers appreciate employees they can trust especially with important projects, issues, and money. Trusted employees get promoted to higher positions to monitor employees and events in the company. You must earn the trust of your employer by showing them you are looking out for their best interests at all times.

- Be someone who works well with others for the good of all. Many companies call this being a "team player" and look for this trait when promoting employees.

- Be the "go to person". If you pay attention to details and listen to others, you will learn valuable information on your job and the operation of the company or organization. If you are the person other employees come to for help, your chances for a promotion are increased.

- Be open to criticism. If you are not doing your job as well as possible and that is brought to your attention, accept the criticism as training and do not get upset. Employers do not like employees who think they are never wrong and tend to pass over those employees for promotions.

- Be cool under pressure. Never display panic or over excitement regarding a problem or event. Try to stay calm and cool and handle a problem smoothly. Employers like to think their employees are able to handle a crisis without a sense of panic and often promote those employees.

- Don't make it known money is your motivation. It is a bad idea to go around saying you need a better paying job. Keep your financial condition or requirements to yourself. Employers shy away from promoting employees who are only out for larger salaries at all costs.

- When given extra work do not complain. Sometimes the extra work is given to determine if an employee can handle the work and get the job done. Being able to handle extra work or pitch in when needed is a trait of employees who get promotions.

- Go the extra mile when working with customers or clients. Many people will take the time to tell your supervisor about excellent service. If your supervisors get compliments on you from customers or clients on a regular basis, you will get noticed by management.

- Express that you like your job and like the company at which you are employed. Disgruntled employees are rarely promoted.

- Help other employees if you have completed your work. Remember you are not out for yourself; you are working and getting paid to look out for your employer. Employees who help their employer achieve goals are always in line for promotions.

- Attend night school or training classes. If you want to get promoted you should also increase your education or knowledge. Learning new ideas is always a good thing.

- Suggest ways to improve the workplace. If your employer has a "suggestion box" and you have a good idea you should think about sharing that idea. Be careful not to suggest risky changes or be offended if the employer decides your suggestion is not needed.

- If you can save the company money you should do so provided you do not do things to hurt the company, their image, or their customer service. The accounting department usually notices a reduction in costs in a department.

- Say nice things about your employer at all times. Things you say will get back to company officials at one time or another so make sure they are good comments.

- Reduce your error rate. Try not to make mistakes at the expense of doing more work. Check your work when possible and if you make a mistake learn from it so you do not repeat the error. Employers prefer fewer errors to more production provided the production is at an acceptable level.

- Never give anyone the impression you would like someone else's job. While you may actually want someone else's job you should keep it to yourself. Good companies do not reward people who try to take the jobs of others.

- If someone is doing something to hurt the employer it is your duty to notify proper management provided you have proof. Companies do not have the time or resources to watch everyone all the time and they depend on their best employees to look out for the company or organization's interests. Few people have managed to obtain promotions by looking the other way when it comes to people hurting the company. When an employee hurts your company by their actions they are also hurting you and everyone else in the company.

- Organize charity events or collections. Most companies ask their employees to donate to charities. People who are willing to take the time to convince others to donate are seen to be leaders and having management potential.

- Be willing to take a temporary position to help the company. One test employers may give to their employees is whether or not the employee is willing to do a different job for the same pay to help the company. In many cases new temporary job duties may become permanent with more pay and possibly management responsibility.

- Bring in treats for fellow employees. Bringing in a box of fresh donuts or cookies will get you noticed by everyone including those who have authority to promote employees. Almost everyone asks who brought in the snacks and if your name is mentioned it goes a long way.

- Always take the time to look good and dress well. Iron your clothes, polish your shoes, and keep your hair groomed well. For men or women, appearance helps people advance in the work place because it shows character, pride, and that the employee cares.

- Personal hygiene is important. Employees who have body odor do not get promoted.

- With women it is especially important that they keep their hair looking good and that they use some, but not too much makeup. Appearance is important for a promotion.

- Always comply with the rules and values of the employer, employers want managers who follow the rules and help achieve the mission and goals of the company or organization.

- Love your job and let it show. Employers promote people who they think will stay with the company and who really like working for the company.
- Think of new ways to make employees happier at their job. New ideas can be as simple as an internal newsletter, banners, awards, employee recognition programs, casual day, or "show and tell" at lunch where employees talk about their hobbies and interests. Once approved by top management, ideas that help productivity result in promotions for those who presented them.
- Offer to pitch in to help the company. As an example, if the lobby needs painting but the company is short on funds to hire a painter, offer to come in on a weekend and use paint provided by the employer to make the lobby look better.

Many employers do not know that the top people and management are watching and looking for employees who go the extra mile for the company or organization without being told to and without complaining.

Promotions don't just happen they are planned, and usually employees are already in line for a promotion even though they do not know it.

Getting along with the boss and co-workers.

No one is saying it is easy to get along with everyone but in the work place it is especially important that you get along.

No one likes to have a boss to tell them what to and when to do it. The concept of a "boss" goes against the DNA of humans. We as people like to be independent and do as we please. The US Constitution guarantees freedoms that we usually have to give up when we enter the workplace and that rubs most people the wrong way. Employees don't vote for their boss, other top people within the organization put the boss in that position.

Like the boss, employees have no real input into who their co-workers are. You can pick your friends, you can pick your teeth, but you can't pick your co-workers (unless you are an independent business person).

Co-workers are just people. For any employee to think their co-workers are somehow different than the rest of the population is not rational. Co-workers have the same characteristics (good and bad) and flaws as the general public. Think of the last time you were at a large gathering such as the fair or a football game. Some people at the event were really nice, some people were not so nice and some people were total jerks. People are people, and your work place is nothing more than a small town with many different types of people and personalities.

One of the main reasons why employees don't like their boss is that they think the boss is picking on them.

To be truthful and fair, in some cases the boss may actually take a dislike to an employee and pick on them. The boss who targets an employee for harassment is an exception and not the norm.

The first thing any employee needs to know about the boss is that the boss may or may not be qualified to be the boss. Sometimes people are promoted for reasons other than their abilities to lead or motivate others.

You can get along with any boss no matter how horrible they are if you take the time to really think over the situation.

Here are some tips for dealing with the boss or improving your relationship with a the boss:

- Always remember the boss is in charge, not you.
- Assume the boss is there because he or she is qualified and has skills that the employer needs.
- Never take job criticism as a personal attack on you. Often when the boss points out problems they are trying to help the employee, not hurt them.

- The boss is human too and may have personal problems that are affecting their attitude. While people (especially the boss) should not bring their problems to work, it happens.
- Bite your tongue. If the boss chews you out, yells at you, or ridicules you in front of others just listen and tell them you will do better. Other employees may be as offended at the boss's actions against you as you are so why make a big deal out of it?
- "I'm on it" is always a good response when the boss asks you to do something. There is no need to make a big discussion out of an assignment or act displeased.
- Compliment the boss. Would it really kill anyone to tell the boss they do a good job or did a good job on a project?
- Thank the boss. Take the time to thank the boss for helping you. The boss has feelings too. Sometimes the reason for a mean boss is that the boss does not feel the employees appreciate the contribution the boss makes to the company and them.
- Stand up for the boss. If other employees trash the boss and you do not feel it is appropriate, take the time to say you do not agree.
- Help the boss. The boss is there to keep things running well which means the company or organization runs well, which means you keep your job. When possible offer to help the boss. Helping the boss will make you feel better about the boss and give the boss a good opinion of you.

- Don't listen to negative people. Negative people tend to say that someone who likes the boss is "sucking up" or "kissing rear". Negative people rarely get promoted, usually do not stay at the same work place, and are usually the first to be laid off. Don't let the negative people drag you down to their level.

- Give the boss a gift on boss's day. A simple gift like a card or a box of donuts can go a long way towards a good relationship with the boss.

- Always think of the boss as a person first and the boss second. Many people who hate their boss will actually start to understand them if they back off and look at the boss as a person and understand the reasons for their stress or attitude. The boss has much higher pressure from the top than the employees they supervise.

- Appreciate the fact that the boss is a shield between you and higher officials. Employees rarely know all the rough meetings the boss went through with their supervisor because of things the employees did.

- Accept the fact that the boss has control over your actions at work. If you think you are more important to the company than your boss, you are mistaken. The boss is there because the company or organization put them there so if sides have to be taken, the company will side with the boss in most cases.

- Take the boss to lunch. Would it really kill you to take the boss to lunch? When employees take the boss to lunch they usually find out the boss is not such a bad person outside of the work place. Even if the boss does not go to lunch, the offer will help your relationship.

- Do what the boss tells you. What a great deal! The boss tells you to do something and if it causes problems the boss is to blame not you, so why would you argue?

- If the boss needs your help give it top priority. It makes sense that if the boss comes to you with something they want done it IS top priority unless they tell you otherwise. Employees should be glad the boss came to them as that reflects that the boss respects their abilities to get the job done, which is a compliment.

- Don't worry about what the boss gets paid. What the boss gets paid does not put food on your table or pay your bills so don't worry about it. Hopefully you might be promoted some day so work towards that goal of being promoted not being jealous of the boss. Jealousy can make people ill.

- Take the time to feel sorry for the boss. If the boss does something wrong or does not meet company goals it would be a lot better to feel sorry for them and try to help them rather than get some type of satisfaction. Feeling good about the boss not doing well will always come back to get you at some point. Not waiting for "Karma" to get you gives you once less thing to worry about at work. What goes around comes around.

- If appropriate, take the time to ask the boss about family. When you are in the boss's office look around for pictures and if you see picture, ask about that person (such as children or spouse). You may find the boss is not at all like you thought they were.

- Never sell out the boss. If there is a problem and you go running to top management you may find you are the one that goes out the door. Top management has little respect for employees who tattle tale on their supervisors unless it is really important or violates major policies or rules. You should talk with the boss before going over their head.

The boss may not be your friend but you must work with them and do what they tell you to at work.

If you cannot find a way to like the boss at least a little, you would probably be happier finding another job.

Co-workers are called co-workers because they work together with you to accomplish a particular goal.

Like the boss, you do not choose your co-workers so you must get along with them. Co-workers are what you make of them. If you spend your time hating co-workers then you will hate your place of employment and your job.

Think back when you were in elementary school or high school. Did you like everyone at your school? Were there people at school that you could not stand? Did some people at school disgust you? Of course you did not like everyone at school so why would you think you would like everyone where you work?

Unlike the boss, having a good relationship with co-workers is easy.

There will be people you really like at work and those you do not like, as that is human nature and cannot be changed. To get along simply socialize with the employees you like and don't socialize with the employees you don't like. If you have to work directly with an employee you do not like, stick to work and don't discuss personal issues, politics, or religion. If an employee feels the need to force their views on you there is the option for you to say you need to get back to work and then you should get back to work.

You should not ignore or be mean to employees or co-workers you do not like and it would be best to treat them as co-workers and try to work with them to get the job done. Usually when someone does not like another person they know it. This is not about your spouse or family member, this is work and you can leave it when you clock out so there is no need to dwell on not liking a fellow employee.

Use some of the same tips above regarding your boss.

If the tension is so high and the work environment so horrible that you cannot stand working with someone you should meet with the boss and ask for move to another department or location. Bosses usually understand that all employees will not get along but you need to be careful not to turn your meeting with the boss into an attack session on another employee.

Time is on your side. If there is an employee that cannot get along with other employees they usually end up out the door or being isolated where they cannot bother anyone.

You couldn't get rid of students you did not like at school so don't think you can get rid of employees you can't get along with.

Like the boss issue, if you have no choice but to work with an employee that drives you crazy you may do best to find another job. Before you take another job give your current employer a chance to re-assign you if you still want to work there.

People are people. The employee you cannot get along with took most of their life getting that way and nothing you do will change them in the relatively short time you will work together.

Making the most of your job.

You found a job, you got the job, and you are doing everything possible to enjoy your job, now what?

Every employee should make the most of their job not for the employer but for their own well being.

First employees need to know that what they do is important. No matter what the job, how low the pay, or how little they seem to be appreciated, their job is important. Companies or organizations are not in the habit of creating jobs just to make jobs. Jobs exist and people get paid because there is a real need for the job.

Most employees would be amazed if they actually took the time to stop and think about how many people their job will impact. It doesn't matter what the job is, the job everyone does will impact a lot of people the employee will never know. The janitor keeps a location clean for all the people who work or visit and they will notice. The factory worker builds items that will be used by other people or other companies who employee people. The service industry keeps track of documents and data that may affect many people, companies, and organizations. The person that washes cars at the dealership makes the purchaser feel good about their new car and helps produce new sales. The stockroom person is so important that the company or organization would come to halt if the job were not there. Any employee who feels what they do in their job is not important is simply mistaken or does not see the whole picture.

Employees should have plans for where they work. They can plan to find ways to make things run smoother, they can plan to move up in the company or organization, or they can plan to be the best they can be at any job.

With unemployment always present in our society, people who have jobs are lucky to have them even in the best of times. The fact that someone has a job says the person is qualified and needed.

Jobs create income for employees and that income pays the bills. Each time an employee gets paid it should remind them of why they work so hard. In many cases the employee may feel they are not paid enough and that may be true, but if we all got paid what we thought we were worth we would all be millionaires.

The working conditions of a job may not be the best but they are what they are. Many times employees may be able to improve their working conditions but for some reason would rather not do anything and would rather complain than try and fix the problems.

Like everything, a job is what a person makes of it. If you think your job is horrible and what you are doing is worthless than your job is worthless to you. If you go to work every day and realize you are needed and your job is important, your job will be important to you.

If a worker hates their job and nothing can change their mind, they should find another job or they will have a miserable career and life.

Make the most of your job and your job will make the most of you!

Being happy at your job.

Being happy at your job is relatively easy and you are in total control of that aspect of your job.

Simple things can make the difference in your being happy at your job or hating where you work.

A few simple things can make your job a happy one and they cost little or nothing.

- Make your work place your own. If possible put posters, plants, pictures, and other items that make you happy at your workstation or desk. If it is allowed, customize your desk to express your feelings. Think of your desk or workstation as an extension of your home and your life. Some people seem to think their job is bad and they do not want to make their workstation look pleasant and that is a huge mistake. Other employees may think they will get another job soon so why bother to take the time to decorate their workstation and that is even a bigger mistake because top people will notice. Sure, there are some companies that do not allow personal effects on a desk or work station but those companies are poorly run and usually have a very high turnover of employees which costs the company a lot of money and profits.

- Wear clothes that make you happy and make you feel good. If you do not have to wear a uniform, wear clothes and colors that give excite you or make you happy. If you do have to wear a uniform wear it with pride and make sure it is crisp and clean and you will feel better. Some jobs require safety helmets and if allowed, purchase or obtain a safety helmet that makes you feel good such as college team or colorful graphics that express your hobbies.

- When you have to go to your job each day be thankful that you have a job (at this time over 10 million Americans are unemployed).

- Take "toys" to work. If you like music, take a device to work so you can use earphones and listen to your favorite music while at lunch. If you have hobbies take magazines to work to read at lunch to take your mind off work during lunch. If you like photography, take a small camera to work and take some pictures of landscaping or other things that might interest you. People with cars they love often take lunch in their car so they can sit in the car and listen to the radio and admire the car.

- Make your lunch or breaks fun. If the weather is nice and you are allowed to do so, take a walk and enjoy the outdoors and fresh air. If you are outside all day at work, go to an eating-place and eat inside so you can enjoy being inside for a while. Eat outside on beautiful days.

- Find someone at work that shares your interests so you can socialize at lunch with a friend.

- While at lunch take the time to call a loved one that should cheer you up and make your workday better.
- Look around at your fellow employees and think of them as people and appreciate them like you would want to be appreciated. Feeling good about your co-workers and the job they do will make you feel good about yourself.
- If someone is giving you a hard time remember that it is their problem not yours, and don't let it bother you.
- Plan things to do on the way home from work. Think of things you enjoy doing and do them after work instead of the weekend, that way you look forward to each workday.
- Be cheerful at work. When one employee is cheerful other employees tend to act the same and the workplace is a better place.
- Don't worry about your job or job security. Many people spend their whole working life worrying about getting fired or laid off. If you get fired or laid off there is nothing you can do about it so don't worry about what might happen. The odds are you will not get laid off or fired. Substitute working towards a promotion in place of worrying about being fired or laid off and you will be a lot happier on and off the job.
- Talk to friends that don't work for your company about their jobs and issues. In many cases your friends may not have it as good as you and that should make you appreciate your job more and make you happier at work.
- Many times the pay is not too low; your spending is too high! Quit wasting money on things you do not need, find ways to

save money, cut your expenses where possible, and pay off and destroy those credit cards. When you get to keep more of the money you work for you are a lot happier at work and at home. It is nice to look at your bank account and actually see the money that came from your paycheck instead of giving it to everyone else.

- Look deep inside yourself with honesty and determine is it really the job that is making you unhappy or is it something else? Many times the job is blamed for unhappiness instead of the real reason. Jobs can't argue or defend themselves from blame. Blaming your job is a great cop-out for not solving problems in your life that you cause or control.

- Exercise at work. Take a walk at lunch to no only make you feel better but to improve your health and to maintain or lose weight. Even on bad weather days, most businesses have halls or buildings where you can walk around for exercise. Some businesses even offer exercise rooms and you should use them.

- Quit beating yourself up. If you are getting up in age and still do not have the dream job you always wanted you should accept your life and look back on the good things and good times where you work. Some things in life are simply beyond your control. Even the worst workplaces have a few good memories, nice people, or funny events. Dwell on good things not bad things.

- Don't smoke, and if you do try to quit. Nicotine makes people hyper and nervous, as does coffee.

- Get an aquarium or a fake pet. If your workplace allows, an aquarium is fun and interesting. If your workplace is not suited to an aquarium, pick out a funny stuffed animal for your desk or workplace. Framed pictures of animals doing funny things tend to calm people and make people laugh.

- Doodle. When things get tough take a few minutes to doodle something funny or of interest to you. Drawing can calm your nerves and funny drawings can make you laugh.

- If you have a good relationship with a client or customer, pick up the phone and call them to see how they are doing and to chat. Not only is calling a favorite client or customer work related socializing, the party you call will really appreciate your call and remember you the next time they need our services or products.

- Travel to favorite places. If your work requires or allows travel, try to save your favorite places for last. If you love the beach and you have a client or customer at the beach you must visit, schedule the visit so you will have something to look forward to at work. On business related trips plan for time to enjoy the trip after you have competed your work. Think of company paid trips to the beach, mountains, new cities, or recreation areas as a company paid vacation with a little work thrown in.

- When you get to work each morning take the time to look at the building, landscaping, scenery, and other employees going to work and admit it is not such a bad place to work. In fact, if you take the time to look at your workplace with open eyes you may realize you have a great job.

- Trust your co-workers. Feel secure knowing that most of your co-workers will be there if you need them for any reason. It is nice to know someone "has your back" and is on your side.

Happiness at the workplace is not the responsibility of the employer. Happiness comes from within a person and is totally under their control. Like life, your job is what you make of it so make it a happy job you enjoy. You have the power, so use it.

Fired, Laid off, Can't get a job?

It can be very depressing to most people when they get fired from a job because they may not realize they are just like everyone else.

Almost everyone at all job levels has either been fired or had to quit a job before they were fired. For some odd reason, society has made people who get fired think they are inferior or different than everyone else when in fact it is just the opposite. Unless you know you did something really stupid and have not changed your attitude, getting fired is not your fault and you should not blame yourself.

There are many reasons for someone to get fired but it really comes down to the employer simply did not like the employee for one reason or another. An employer will do everything possible to keep from firing someone they like. Sometimes the employee gets fired because their boss does not like them and never has from day one. Other times an employee might get fired because a relative of a company official or a friend needs their job. The worst and a common reason to fire someone is to not have to pay unemployment like the company would have if they simply laid the person off as planned due to financial problems at the company or organization.

Getting fired or terminated is easy. The employer can think up a "million" reasons to fire someone even reasons that make no sense at all can be used to terminate an employee. How many times have you heard a boss tell someone they don't like their looks right before they tell them they are fired? It actually does happen. Some of the latest and dumbest reasons for terminating an employee are; that the employee is a smoker, the employee has two jobs, the employee is not a "team player" (is work a football team? Who knew!), the employee just "doesn't fit in" (whatever that means), and any other silly excuse the employer can think of to free up a job position for whatever reason. If you follow the tips earlier in this book you may have a better chance of not being fired even if the reason is totally stupid.

Some people really do deserve to get fired because they come to work drunk, take drugs, don't work, show up late, do sloppy work, or any of the other things people would not tolerate from their children or family, much less an employee.

Whether you deserve to be fired or not is not the issue. If you are fired there are some things you can do to help get another job.

Any attorney will tell you there is the truth and there is attorney truth. What does that mean? As an example, on applications it asks if you have ever been terminated or forced to resign from a job. If you were terminated you could answer yes and not be considered for a job. There is another truthful way to answer the question using "attorney truth". If you are terminated, immediately tell the person firing you that you quit five minutes ago and that way you can truthfully say you were not terminated on any application. If the potential employer calls your past employer and they tell them you were terminated (which may be a violation of privacy laws) and the potential employer gives you a chance to explain, tell them you quit and the employer must have said you were fired so they would have to pay unemployment. Both statements would be true in a way.

If you were fired from a job and have a time frame where you show no job, show that you were self-employed. Never show time on your application where you show no work. Employers get suspicious of people who have gaps in their employment history. Right after being fired go around offering to mow people's yards or trim their shrubs that way you can put down "self employed landscaping business" for the time you were not working for a company. The company looking to hire you may actually be impressed you are not afraid of hard work. If the potential employer asks for names of clients give them name of friends you can trust (and have told in advance) as references. Using "attorney truth" if you snipped one little piece of a shrub at your friend's place even with your finger, you trimmed their shrub and if you cut a blade of grass with a pocket knife, you cut their grass.

The worst things you can do if you are fired are to go crazy, hit the boss, or cause a scene. If you get arrested after being fired you now have an arrest record for assault at work and your time working for anyone may be over.

If you really want to get even with your employer who fires you, be nice to them. After they notify you that you are fired or terminated you should tell them you enjoyed working for them, you liked your job, you liked the people, and you really appreciate the opportunity. Those comments will accomplish several things. First you have stunned the person firing you as if you punched them in the face since they did not expect that response. Second, if they fired you to make you suffer or harass you, the joke is on them because it did not work out the way they expected. Third, if you get fired and leave on good and friendly terms many employers will not tell another employer you were fired an may actually say nice things about you or tell you about jobs at other companies.

Take the high road when terminated, show the company you have dignity and class and you might just ruin their plans for you.

If you have been laid off, you are among only a few people if you consider almost a hundred million people over 20 years a few people. In fact if you do not get laid off at least once in your working career you are truly a rare individual.

Usually people who get laid off knew in advance it might be coming so at least they have a chance to find another job and quit before they are laid off. Unfortunately executives of companies have a bad habit of lying to their employees about the stability of the company so they can have time to find other jobs for themselves. While it won't help pay your bills, there should be some comfort in knowing that if the top executives knew what they were doing and were actually worth their big paycheck the company would not have fallen apart and no one would have been laid off.

It is not the fault of employees when they get laid off so no employee should blame himself or herself or feel bad when they are laid off from a job.

People who have been laid off actually have a better chance at getting a job than those who have a job and are looking to change jobs. Human resource managers and people doing the hiring feel sympathy and know how it feels because they also may have been laid off at one time or another or they know someone who has. Don't act ashamed of being laid off.

Layoffs come in cycles and no company or organization is exempt. Even the military, police, fire departments, universities, hospitals, and so called "recession proof" organizations or companies have had to reduce their employee numbers at times.

In these times layoffs are just a fact of life so don't let it bother you.

Can't get a job?

Everyone will eventually find a job. No matter how unskilled or skilled they are, how young or old they are, or what they look like, there is a job out there for everyone. The job a person finds may not be their dream job or may not have the highest pay, but it is a job and the road to advancement to other jobs. Think of any job you take in an emergency as either training for advancement within the organization or a source of income until you find that job you really want. It is easier to get a job when you have one than when you don't have a job.

Temporary and part time jobs are great ways to get into an organization and show them what you can do. Most companies use temporary job agencies as a way to bring a person into the workforce and to see if they fit in without any strings attached. If the person sent by the temp agency does not fit his or her needs, the requesting manager simply asks the agency to send someone new. Once the company finds a temporary employee that they like, they almost always offer them the next open job for which they are qualified. The same goes for part time jobs.

There is more good news.

If you really think about it, you will realize you do not know of anyone who was laid off or fired from a job that was not better off eventually.

Right now you know someone that was laid off or fired, found a new job or career, and is making more money and happier than when they were laid off.

In one particular case several employees who were laid off at a corporation found new careers making more money than the top management who laid them off.

Many laid off employees have relocated to other areas only to ask themselves why they did not move there along time ago since they like it so much.

Some people use being laid off or fired as a reason to follow their dreams and do something they have wanted to do all their life but did not because they didn't want to lose their job. Starting a small business is the most common dream that is realized from people being fired of laid off.

If you feel the world is against you, recall the saying earlier in this book "they can kill you but they can't eat you". Nothing is more satisfying than getting even with those who tried to hold you down than for you to rise up even better than you were before.

Jobs are the easiest things to find in the world and there are always plenty of them. Be patient, it may take a while to find a job but you will find one and you will survive.

Do your best, use the tips in this book, work hard, and don't let anyone or anything get you down. Things will work out for you if you have a positive attitude and give it your best. I know it's true, I have seen it a lot times and I have been there.

About the author

Mark Kirby is a recognized management, employee retention, and efficiency expert with almost thirty years combined experience in the following fields:

- Executive management experience including supervision of management staff, hiring, recruiting employees, employee retention, employee wellness, job position creation, and employee benefits.
- Customer service staff management
- Investigation staff management
- Financial Management
- Audit staff management
- Author of multiple books
- Guest columnist for a newspaper

- Safety program management
- Risk Management
- Actuarial and Premium calculation
- Computer program automation of premium calculation and the claims handling and reserving process for a large insurance carrier.
- Guest speaker for organizations and associations.
- Management and staff training supervisor
- Digital product sales and consulting
- Management and employee wellness consultant

Mr. Kirby has also been published in an international insurance publication, and has given many lectures on Worker's Compensation.

Many businesses and agencies have credited Mr. Kirby with saving their business due to management issues or greatly reducing costs without reducing employees.

In addition, Mr. Kirby was greatly instrumental in rescuing an insolvent Insurance Carrier and changing the 30 million dollar shortfall in the claims fund to a surplus.

Mr. Kirby has also appeared on a national talk radio show.

Mr. Kirby has also worked in the past as a retail clerk, construction helper, carpenter's apprentice, janitor, car restoration specialist, garment printer, car rental clerk, and many other jobs that taught him that all jobs are important and that no job makes a person better than anyone else.

Mark Kirby wishes you the best and he can be contacted by mail at:

Mark Kirby
President/CEO
PO Box 6517
Columbia, SC 29260-6517

Please note due to the volume of mail Mr. Kirby receives he may not be able to respond to all letters however your comments are important to him.

Note: This sample resume/letter will fit on a single 8.5 X11" page.

John Doe
555 Maple Street
Any City, USA 22222
555-555-5555

RESUME

Qualifications:

- Graduate of The University of State
- B.S. Degree in Business Administration
- 10 years experience in Management, Safety, Employee Supervision, Customer Service, Procurement, and Sales for a major corporation
- Currently unemployed and working part time due to being laid off

Abilities and Traits:

- Technically oriented and easy to train.
- Open to new ideas and careers.
- Dependable, loyal, and dedicated employee.
- Ability to work well with people.
- Friendly and easy going.
- Not afraid to do a "hands on" job.

Type of position sought:

I will consider any openings at your company. I am always interested in new job experiences for which I am qualified. A full time position is best, however I would be willing to accept a part time or temporary position. The salary or job title is not as important to me as a good work environment and working with a top company.

Please call, email, or write me regarding any job openings at your organization. I would like very much to apply in person.

Thank you for your time and consideration, I look forward to hearing from you.

Very truly yours,

John Doe
Johndoe@doemail.com
555-555-5555

Job Notes:

1. Company name

2. Job Opening Title

3. Salary

4. Date applied and resume sent (specify each)

5. Application submission date

6. Contact person and their title

7. Contact phone number

8. Contact email address

9. Results of job interest

10. Follow up dates

11. Results of follow ups:

12. Describe workplace environment

13. Considered or not considered for the job

14. List any referrals to other jobs

15. Describe feelings about the job and company

www.ingramcontent.com/pod-product-compliance
Lightning Source LLC
Chambersburg PA
CBHW072040190526
45165CB00018B/1189